OF HI

Den

ISBN: 978-1-913642-30-3

Book designed by Aaron Kent

Edited by Aaron Kent

Broken Sleep Books (2021), Talgarreg, Wales

Contents

Of Hearts

Karen Dennison

At Point Nemo

At the height of youth, I circled earth.
It spun at my feet, a distant beauty;
admirers attracted into graveyard orbits.

For me the sun was another star
and though I learnt its physics,
I worshipped it as Ra, studied its secrets.

I was unbreakable and made of light
and time was for other people. I witnessed
the fall of *peace* - Mir breaking up

on re-entry with smoking hands and fireball-
fingertips, crashing into the South Pacific.
My own descent into waves was sudden,

knocked off course by junk and debris.
For decades I lay on the seabed
with other wrecks and remnants of life.

Diving down through miles of water,
you swam into the sunken city of my heart,
emptied my drowned mouth. I listened

to your stories of the surface, began to believe
in rebirth, in escaping gravity's grip on my bones;
felt like I was back in high orbit. But you left

how you arrived — a lone explorer on a mission,
fearless. And every night is terminal velocity,
nothing but the cemetery to break my fall.

***

*"Point Nemo" (oceanic pole of inaccessibility) is the area of ocean
furthest from land and is the location of the so-called Spacecraft
Cemetery where retired spacecraft are sent.*

Winter's story

High-rise lights are swallowed by night,
        station lamps planetary in blackness;
platforms sacrifice themselves to cold.
        Windows are mirrors to a self who lives in glass,
in broken moments, inventing a narrative
        for the time that's lost.

When trees are dusk's dreams and voices
        a distant hum, earth draws the sky around herself,
a scarf beaded with stars, the simplest things she knows.
        I sift the day through tired thoughts,
let it drift, live on the edges of things,
        lightly tethered to the lip of the world.

Sorrow unbuttons her throat, throws her white coat
        on the ground. The air is naked sadness;
nothing remains untouched by her skin.
        She gives me snow, abandons
herself from cloud. I know she wants to show me
        the opposite of warmth, the end of love.

I walk home with uncertain feet, fingers cold;
        slabs of ice splintering over patches
of pavement. In this glittering, I am young,
        forget how broken I have become.
Waking to another slow dark morning
        I count the days that run away like children.

After you're gone

I scour dead light,
      coded impulses hurtling
through blood-dark space;
      island suns that broadcast
their lonely semaphore.

My heart's a pulsar
      sweeping the night,
warm breath on cold glass
      condensing to gas clouds,
constellations.

I search until
      the stars switch off
and the shore of sky
      weathers your bones to dust.

My island

I close my eyes, travel to a place where
there's no boundary between skin
and air, where thoughts must rise
and disappear like hot-air balloons
tear-dropping limitless skies.

The hardest furthest part of the journey
is letting go, untethering you from my heart,
from my skin. An open flame burns
in my eyes. Alone on the shoreline,
I feel you leave and leave and leave.

Between the lines

White spaces are ghosted words
where I lifted my pen,
unwrote sorrow's wrist,

sewed up my lips. In the gaps,
my quiet hands unravel the sky
of that summer, stretch it

over the miles earth has spun
between now and then, throw dust
in my eyes. Pale skin lies across

the page; letters fallen from creased
palms anchor themselves in my heart.
My empty lines, scarred with loss,

pick at invisible seams, unstitch
the darkness I've been holding in.

Heart in my mouth

This is what my heart knows
– the weight of words,
blind-embossed on its walls.

And down in the hollowed out
calyx is the echo-chamber
of a ghost-pulse, still-born heart.

Rose-hip exposed, the stem
from a buried seed rises up my throat,
heart-blooms in my mouth.

And when I open my lips
to speak, petals
fly out.

The Impossible Museum

Enter the dome-roofed room
full of still-born words,
a universe of every unvoiced thought.

Pick up headphones and hear
the never-still brain whirr, watch on repeat
the broken images of dreams.

Peer through a chest-high cabinet of glass,
as wide as outstretched arms,
that holds a day's worth of exhaled breath.

Draw aside black curtains to witness
a love that ricochets in the cave of a skull,
never sees the light of day.

In the gift shop, purchase a vial of grief.
Drink it, if you dare, to feel it rattle
the prison door of another's ribs.

Moon song

At night she's a lidless eye watching our dreams
projected onto windows, walls. She enters
our arenas of fear, of large and small spaces,
immeasurable heights and falling.

She knows the destitute, the homeless, feels
their dust-cold shivers in her empty seas, drips
her thought-tears on midnight, all-night, drunks;
sings with them their songs, silently, silverly.

She longs for foxes to shadow her rocks; stuttering moths
and shape-shifting bats to shelter in her craters.
Sometimes she sees her face drowning in water,
as if contorted in a circus mirror.

It's then she catches sight of the blackness at her back
she's slowly falling into. And she knows what it means
to die, to grieve for earth's dark beating heart.

Hollow hours

Against the backdrop of memory,
spotlights zig-zag up cliffs of darkness,
weathered by thoughts that tailspin
down tunnels of night.

Lit up like rain in headlights,
each circle's the full moon,
a dying month. Behind its face,
this curdling blackness where images
pattern the dark, brief as sparklers.

Sleep, locked out, whines
like a tethered dog. Gloom stretches me
on its rack until the sun's long fingers
untie my wrists, conjure illusions
of light, make me forget.

Cast adrift

Houses huddle
like cows in rain. Clouds
free-roam.

The track has laid itself down,
stretched on the rack
of land.

My eyes roll down its spine.
There is no stopping, sky
closing in.

Sun at one o'clock pierces
the window, needles
into my skin,

pins me to each moment
like muscle to bone.

Toward eternity

I'm forever walking down the unlit road,
torch in hand, tunneling limitless dark.
It's always night and shadows pass,
throw themselves to the ground.

I step on their soft heartless skin
and they unpeel at my back, wrap
their wings around my neck. It's cold
and the sky denies me its stars.

I am small as a stone and the air
in my lungs is hiding what it knows.
And in every leaf there's a dying breath
and in every breath an unearthed seed.

At the edge

Clouds are fading in the river's channel
like the memory of your face. Aeroplane trails
criss-cross summer skies, dissolve to vapour blue.

I'll find you where the sun's rays walk on water,
leave blinding footprints. I dip my fingers
into liquid silver that parts, shivering,

and your hand slips in mine, pulls me under.

Epicentre of Longing

Longing begins in bone,
permeates blood,
fills lungs,

ruptures my body
with breath. It rises
with sun-warmed winds,

flies over continents, sinks
down a rift. This longing
shadows a fault-line,

ghost of an earthquake, stretches
across the sea-bed,
grounds itself

on the shore of your heart,
shaken by a tsunami
of grief.

Little Compton

I'll stash the old cassette, that soundtrack you made me,
in my heart. I'll rest my heart on the bench
of stone in the terracotta chapel where we sat
in its circular silence, read about a monument to love.

I'll shrink the chapel down
so it fits on my palm, tie it to a rock, row a boat
out to the Surrey lake. As I reach out, offer the chapel
to its waters, its skin will shudder and break, then heal

the wound it makes. The little chapel will sink
to its bed and years of lake will rock my heart
to sleep and my heart will dream of your music,
unspooling from its tape.

Here again

The lapping of the sea was a hand
throwing stars that shone white
in the daytime sky.

Hand-in-hand with summer, I ran
on a cliff-top of soft moss, green smiling
for miles. Our sun shook like a tambourine,
golden notes drifting to the ground.

The scent of jasmine was restless as a swallow,
its trail an after image of scissoring wings.
It led me to a secret river where I dipped my feet
in ripples of sound, heard your voice
darting in and out, hummingbird-green.

Days like these

It's days like these, the first to gather
        a harvest of sun, that I need

to forget, just lie down. I need the ticking
        of leaves to echo in my rib-cage,

for brambles to cut your face from my eyes.
        I need to stitch up the hole with threads

of breeze, cauterise the wound with ageless light.
        I need the buzz of newly woken bees

to seize your name from my tongue,
        for the sky to mend my foolish heart.

Immanence

Nothing right now is louder than rain
as if all the pebbles from Brighton Beach
have catapulted from the sky, each one
hitting the bullseye of a thought;

each thought like a fragile glass, each rim
circled by a licked finger, waves resonating
into one repeating wordless sound.

Under its weight, leaves mouth their hymn
struck by stony drops, hold out tongues
in communion. And as the seed of a blackbird's prayer
begins to grow, it's snatched by a river cascading

down the roof of the house, diving from its gutters.
My reflection wavers from a watery other-world,
submerged, unreal; signals like a deep sea diver.

Between cloud

There's a broken sky, a ragged arc
inside banks of stratocumulus.

Shadow-black houses hide their hearts,
their hurt. The split horizon

lifts me up, leaf-light. And nothing
matters except the blue-glow line suturing

the sky and how my body has finally
healed the wounds of loss,

and grief is sleeping, curled up
in the gap between clouds.

Acknowledgements

Poems from this collection, or versions of them, have previously been published in *Riggwelter, erbacce, Reliquiae, The Lake,* and *Poetry Village*. At the edge was written in response to artwork by Linda Arkley and features in the poetry/art anthology *Stone's Throw* (published by Colchester Mosaic Stanza group).

Toward Eternity takes its name from the final words of the poem *Because I could not stop for Death* by Emily Dickinson.

LAY OUT YOUR UNREST

Lightning Source UK Ltd.
Milton Keynes UK
UKHW020731040121
376155UK00004B/155